WHALE HUNTERS WISDOM SERIES
Volume I

MIND OF A HUNTER

Cultivate Your Company's Strategic Sales Mentality

Dr. Barbara Weaver Smith
and The Whale Hunters

The Whale® Hunters

**BIGGER DEALS
BIGGER CUSTOMERS**

www.thewhalehunters.com
© 2007-2016 The Whale Hunters, Inc.

info@thewhalehunters.com

Whale Hunters Wisdom Series

By Dr. Barbara Weaver Smith
and The Whale Hunters

Volume I

Mind of a Hunter: Cultivate Your Company's Strategic Sales Mentality

Volume II

The Hunt: Strengthen Your Sales Process to Accelerate Business Growth

Volume III

Riding the Whale: Adapt Your Sales Strategies to Close Big Deals

Volume IV

The Whale Hunting Culture: Engage Your Entire Company in Business Development

info@thewhalehunters.com

www.thewhalehunters.com

ISBN: 978-0-9822091-8-9

Published in the United States of America by The Whale Hunters, Inc.

The Whale Hunters
3054 East Bartlett Place
Chandler, AZ 85249
www.thewhalehunters.com
info@thewhalehunters.com

480.584.4012

Preface

Aimed at owners and executives seeking explosive growth for their companies, the *Whale Hunters Wisdom* series offers explanations, tools, personal anecdotes and real life examples to guide you in scouting, hunting, and harvesting "whales," those accounts 10 to 20 times larger than your current average account.

The Whale Hunters Process™ is derived from our study of how the Inuit people of far northwestern Alaska hunted whales. Their story is one of indomitable courage and persistence. A small team of people ventured out into icy waters in a sealskin boat during the dark days of early Spring to capture and then land and harvest the biggest mammal on earth. Their story has the power of truth, and we have great respect and admiration for the Inuit. The dangerous hunt demanded tremendous courage, a special boat and tools, and a ritual that ensured the hunters and villagers would be successful. Why did the whale hunters risk their lives? **One whale will feed the village for an entire year.**

The Whale Hunters, Inc. is a strategic sales and business development company. We teach a process to develop a fast-growth culture within your company. This permanent process integration requires a defined strategy with clear steps, teamwork, defined responsibilities, and a common understanding that the village survives because it hunts.

Through The Whale Hunters Process™, your company will be positioned for explosive growth that can be managed consistently as you land and support whale-sized accounts. Learn more by visiting our website, www.thewhalehunters.com, where you may register to receive the *Whale Hunters Wisdom* newsletter. It's absolutely free.

info@thewhalehunters.com

www.thewhalehunters.com
© 2007-2016 The Whale Hunters, Inc.

The Whale Hunters Process™
A proven, nine-phase process for transforming sales development

Whale Hunting creates a disciplined sales culture in your company that allows you to optimize your ability to land and harvest large accounts. This dramatic shift in thinking and practice precipitates explosive growth of your company's revenues and market position.

Scouting guides you to know, seek and harpoon whales whose business will be ideal for you. It all starts with knowing who you're hunting, with a focus on market and sales research and the creation of a target filter.

Harvesting brings sales and operations departments together in an integrated process to ensure you harvest your whale effectively, efficiently and harmoniously. It includes key account management and growing new business with your best accounts.

Hunting focuses on communicating with, presenting to, and securely closing your ideal whale accounts. Our method of progressive discovery and disclosure relies on critical questions at each step of the hunt.

V

. . . .

Table of Contents

info@thewhalehunters.com   www.thewhalehunters.com

© 2007-2016 The Whale Hunters, Inc.

Introduction

Whale hunting is not for losers, negative thinkers, or nostalgic dreamers. Eight people set out in a six-foot-long boat made of cypress wood and covered in sealskin. Their target was the largest mammal on earth—the whale—an animal that may weigh over 40 tons and be 50 feet long. A whale's skin can be one foot thick, so it takes great strength and skill to pierce it with a harpoon. Once the harpoon was set in the whale's side, the whale could take the boat with its eight hunters to watery graves. The whale can dive or the line can weaken. Those responsible for controlling the tension on the line can become distracted and allow the whale to release itself.

The minds of the whale hunters cannot drift from their task, even though they may ride the whale for days. To do so invites ruin on themselves, their fellow oarsmen, and the village that is depending on the whale for the next year's sustenance. How the ancient whale hunters' shoulders must have ached, and how they must have longed for anything to break the agony of holding that rope.

So it is for companies embarking on whale hunts. The minds of the hunters must be attuned to the tasks at hand and to the environment surrounding them. The cold, icy water is the whale's home, and he can survive there. Eight men capsized from their boat cannot.

Landing a whale, an account that is 10 to 20 times larger than your current average account, is different from any other kind of sales activity. It requires the concerted effort of many people within your company and the unwavering commitment of the management team and all whale hunters involved.

This volume of the *Whale Hunters Wisdom* series reinforces the need for focus and commitment during a whale hunt. Each of your villagers must know what each Inuit whale hunter knew: the whale is worth the trouble. No amount of distraction, fear, boredom, nostalgia, or other negativity can be allowed to clutter the minds of the whale hunters eager to capture the account that will move your company rapidly to its next vital level.

To read the full whale hunting story, point your web browser to http://thewhalehunters.com/about-us/the-whale-hunters-story/.

3

Numerous warning bells ring as you draw near to the edge of No Man's Land. To continue to grow, you will need to make major changes in your business and your perspective – chief among them, focus.

4

info@thewhalehunters.com

Are You on the Edge of No Man's Land?

Certain critical points in a business's development demand dramatic, transformational change in order to break through to a sustainable and profitable larger size.

We observe those "breaking points" to occur somewhere around the levels of $10 million, $25 million, and $100 million in revenue. Although the numbers are arbitrary, on average they represent the revenue size at which organizations that made the break-through had to significantly change the way that they understood their business.

Fewer than 1.5% of all companies in the United States grow beyond $25 million in annual revenue. In other words, the vast majority of companies never learn to cross "No Man's Land."

We understand that industries, markets, and firms differ, and that our breakpoint revenue amounts are only guidelines. We do believe, however, that if your company is to continue to grow you will reach the edge of "No Man's Land." And when you do, you will need major changes.

How will you know?

Warning Signs:

- **New faces.** You are finding new competitors, smaller, lesser-known firms, in the opportunities that you are pursuing.

5

- **Thunder without rain.** You are swamped by what seem to be new RFPs, and while you have made your way onto the list of qualified companies who bid out large business, you remain too small to win.

- **Red flags.** Bigger players are moving into your niche and perhaps claiming your niche.

- **Bobbing in the ocean.** Annual revenues go up and down like a buoy over several years and you perceive a ceiling of revenue amount that you cannot break through.

- **Trading places.** Your company is losing large accounts at a rate similar to the rate you are adding new ones.

What will you do?

Most companies respond to this lack of traction as they approach "No Man's Land" with one of three responses:

- Change organization chart – reorganize your team hoping for greater productivity

- Change staff – trade out who you consider to be your lowest performers

- Change scope – shift product mix, market, message, or a combination of all three

6

Many of my clients have tried all of these approaches. The results were not great because they were responding to the growth information with structure rather than focus. They did not understand that their company was not necessarily broken; it was just in very different waters from where they had been before.

Our key recommendations:

1. **Fathom your new waters.** You are now in a new world of opportunity. You will be competing against companies much bigger than yours, and yet you will still have your old competitors as well. To win, you will have to learn how to beat the big competitors.

2. **Focus on understanding.** This is not the time to dramatically shift markets. At the edge of "No Man's Land," you are very probably in the right market; however, you have the wrong message and inferior process to deliver it in order to win.

3. **Fashion formal sales processes and measurement.** Because you are in new waters, you need to take a much more scientific approach to determine what the data of the marketplace are telling you. Develop your process for approaching the new, larger opportunities and then make certain that you measure your success in each of the steps of your new approach.

If you can see the signs of "No Man's Land" in your company, it is a good thing. You are on the edge of great opportunity. However, 98.5% of the companies out there can never break through. You will need a plan.

Is it time now to accelerate your passage across "No Man's Land"?

Reflection

Here are some signs of approaching No Man's Land in my company:

New competitors...

Too small to win.

Bigger players in our niche.

Revenue yo-yo.

Trading accounts—not really growing.

8

Action

Here are five steps we could take to better position against new competitors:

1.

2.

3.

4.

5.

Our most important next step is _____

_____

_____

Action steps: For each one,

Who is in charge?

What action should be taken?

When should it be completed?

9

www.thewhalehunters.com

As you prepare to lead your company across No Man's Land – dangerous terrain requiring speedy passage for your very survival – you have several choices. Whale Hunting offers multiple advantages over typical strategies. Find out why.

Crossing No Man's Land

Fewer than 1.5% of all companies in the United States ever grow above $25 million in annual sales. That means that 98.5% of the companies never break through the glass ceiling of being a "small company." Top CEOs who have led companies to huge growth will identify $25 million in annual revenues and then $100 million in annual revenues as significant touch points that required them to manage transformational change in their companies.

However, even understanding this pattern and being able to identify the points in time that you have to change your business in order to grow, the vast majority of business owners and leaders cannot make the change and thus will never grow beyond $25 million.

We call this period of time and revenue growth – between $25 million and $100+ million – "No Man's Land." It's tough terrain to cross.

Consider these distinctions between a $25 million and a $100 million company.

Several characteristics describe the majority of companies in the $25 million revenue size:

- **Market is "niche market."** You have carved out a limited, specific market by product, geography, service offering, or some other characteristic.

- **Sales approach is "avoidance."** You sell below the radar and avoid selling head-to-head against the much larger national firms and industry leaders.

- **Value proposition is "better."** You demonstrate an incrementally better set of benefits in your offering to customers in contrast to your competitors.

But when your company exceeds $100 million in size, the characteristics are different:

- Market is "broad market." You sell a complete, integrated solution to large clients.

- Sales approach is "confrontation." You must face other large competitors head-on in price, integrated solution, technology, service, innovation, and other criteria.

- Value proposition is "completeness." You are expected to provide a complete solution at a very price-competitive rate.

As you begin to cross that space you are significantly at risk. You are becoming too big to hide, yet you still feel too small to fight. Specifically, to attain this level of growth, a company needs to add larger accounts than it did when it was much smaller. This need pushes the smaller company into the marketplace of the larger competitors. Those larger competitors have the option to be very aggressive in "their market" in how they deal with a smaller, up-and-coming firm. They can command resources, technology, broader service base, and possibly price.

So the growing company with aspirations to become much larger than $100 million in revenue needs to cross "No Man's Land" as fast as possible to minimize its vulnerability.

12

You have four options for speedy travel. Here are the first three:

- Acquisition or merger. Buy, merge, or be bought in order to achieve size, capital, and leverage.

- New products. Bet the farm on the introduction of a new product/service for rapid growth.

- New markets. Rapidly expand into markets in which you have little presence with the expectation of high sales volume.

These three options pose the following challenges: they demand significant financial investment; they require a significant distraction from your current client base; and, based upon business statistics, they have a low probability of success.

The fourth option is whale hunting. You probably know by now that by whale hunting we mean the organized and process-driven effort to scout, hunt, and harvest very large accounts. This approach provides multiple advantages over the other three, including:

- Using your current resources rather than undertaking an enormous increase in expense

- Creating a process and implementation methodology that will sustain the business after it has reached its initial growth targets

info@thewhalehunters.com
www.thewhalehunters.com
© 2007-2016 The Whale Hunters, Inc.

- Incorporating predictability and measurement to the achievement of goals throughout the growth process

- Ensuring scalability so that as you grow, you do not need to reinvent the "success magic," but rather your processes are designed to anticipate and accommodate growth

We don't pretend that whale hunting is easy or that you can build a whale hunting culture into your business overnight.

But consider this: whale hunting is not a parable or a fairy tale. It is the true story of how people of indomitable spirit set out with rudimentary tools and technologies to capture the largest mammal on earth in order to ensure that their village survived and thrived.

Are you a whale hunter?

Visit our website now to claim your free list of 50 sample criteria to define your ideal customers!
http://thewhalehunters.com/ideal

14

Reflection

Even if I'm not at $25 million yet, I have these signs of an upcoming No Man's Land:

☐ Revenue has hit a plateau

☐ I am seeing new, bigger competitors

☐ My team's skills are outgrowing our customers' needs

☐ We need to do Something Else in order to keep growing, but I'm not sure what it is!

☐ Our market is changing.

☐ We are getting squeezed on price more than ever.

☐ Other _____

☐ Other _____

15

Action

1. What could we do to begin to expand our niche market?

_____

_____

_____

_____

2. How could we make an existing product or service more marketable by providing extra value?

_____

_____

_____

_____

3. How could we improve our value proposition?

_____

_____

_____

_____

Have you recently refused to turn down business that is no longer appropriate for the company you are becoming? If your self-perception hasn't grown alongside your business, it's time now to break the "minnow mindset." Find out how.

17

Only a Minnow in a Sea of Whales

When my son Brad was in kindergarten, his teacher left the room briefly one afternoon. While she was gone, a couple of sixth graders stopped into the kindergarten room and teased the children. Brad came home in tears.

"I'm never going to sixth grade!" he cried.

"Why not?" I asked him.

"Because they're so big!"

Brad suddenly had a terrifying vision of his future: one little five-year-old in a classroom of big, scary sixth graders! He didn't understand that all of the little kids would grow up together and become the sixth grade meanies!

At The Whale Hunters, we find a similar type of misunderstanding among business owners. It's a mindset that makes you feel small even as your customers and competitors have grown bigger and meaner. We hear you express this fear as a refusal to turn down business that is no longer essential, profitable, or suitable for the company you are becoming. You have grown as big and as important as all the other sixth graders, but your self-perception hasn't grown alongside your business.

18

Do you ever feel like a minnow in a sea of whales?

Here are some give-away comments:

- "It's not a great deal for us, but the customer is prestigious."

- This customer may be too small for us today, but we'd better take them because they might get big later."

- "We can't turn down this deal; the customer is influential in our marketplace."

- "We've built this business on doing the things that bigger companies turn down!"

How do you break the minnow mindset?

The consequences of this misunderstanding can be deadly to your business. Instead of doing bigger deals, better deals, and more profitable deals to feed your growth, you run the risk of devoting too much attention and too many resources to a growing number of accounts that are too small for you.

Our key recommendations:

- Outsource smaller accounts to a strategic partner

- Develop your target filter for new customers in terms of criteria that will feed your growth

- Measure and re-assess how your business makes money

- Map your sales processes to meet your criteria

- Manage your sales organization to achieve evolving company goals

Can you cast aside the minnow mindset?

Visit our website now to claim your free list of 50 sample criteria to define your ideal customers!
http://thewhalehunters.com/ideal

20

Reflection

Do I have a minnow mindset? What are the things I do or say that reveal I am thinking too small?

_____

_____

_____

_____

_____

_____

_____

How would my whale hunts change if I allow myself to say no to all the things that are too small or insignificant?

_____

_____

_____

_____

_____

_____

_____

_____

info@thewhalehunters.com

www.thewhalehunters.com
© 2007-2016 The Whale Hunters, Inc.

Action

What assignments, jobs, tasks or sales could I outsource?

_____

_____

_____

What is the minimum size of deal I will do in the future?

_____

_____

_____

How do I measure profitably?

_____

_____

_____

What is one opportunity to which I will say NO?

_____

_____

What changes do I need to make in how I manage The Whale Hunting Process™?

_____

_____

22

Maybe you think of your brand as your logo, or your tagline, or even your product or packaging, but your customers think of your brand as a promise—what do you promise them in exchange for their money? All of your success is tied to the strength and validity of that promise—so read this chapter to check it out!

23

How to Audit Your Brand Promise

Whale Hunting begins with clarifying your brand promise—what are your most compelling promises to your prospective customers? Can you simply and clearly differentiate your value proposition from those of your competitors? When I work with companies, usually we discover that the brand promise is less "unique" than they thought—they are not distinctly separating out the "standard promises" – those that everyone in their business makes – from the true distinctive of their company, products, or services.

Here's a way to test this premise in your company and also provide a road map for improvement. We call it a **Brand Promise Audit**.

1. Gather marketing information from your company and at least three competitors. Print pages from their website and other marketing materials. Make several copies of each collection.

2. With your cross-functional team, ask everyone to browse through one set of materials with a pack of sticky notes handy. They should write down "brand promises" that they read in the materials, putting only one promise statement on each sticky note. Label the note "X" for a competitor and your company's initials for your statements.

3. Place the brand promises on one, two, or three flip charts (with 4-5 people working at a flip chart). When everyone has finished browsing materials, gather at the flip charts. Reorganize the notes, collecting all of the similar statements one on top of another.

24

4. With one person recording on another flip chart, make a list of all the brand promises that are repeated several times. These represent "standard promises." Your competitors make the same statements that you do. All of your customers expect these benefits. They constitute the price of admission.

Here's an example of **Standard Benefits**:

- We are a partner with you.

- We react quickly to changes.

- We promise excellent service.

- Our product/service is cost effective.

- We have a courteous, well-trained staff.

- Our processes are certified.

- Our company is an industry leader.

- We exceed your expectations.

- We are ROI-driven.

- We deliver on time and on budget.

- We are innovative.

Although these particular examples come from the marketing materials of Call Centers, notice that they could represent almost any product or service. They are completely nondescript and, therefore, almost meaningless to your customers.

Your team may also want to argue, "Well, everybody SAYS that but we really DO it!" If you decide that's true, then you will need to do a very specific and clever job of marketing how you exceed your competitors' claims in one or more areas.

WHALE HUNTERS WISDOM SERIES: MIND OF A HUNTER How to Audit Your Brand Promise

. . . .

5. Next, record a list of your competitors' statements that are not often repeated. Do a second list of your company's statements that are not often duplicated. On each of these lists, cross out any statements that the team finds unimportant.

6. What's left is a list of somewhat distinctive claims or statements that YOU make and that YOUR COMPETITORS make to customers. These may be Superior Benefits.

Here's an example of **Superior Benefits**: (again from the call center industry)

- We specialize in bilingual call center services (English and Spanish) for the healthcare industry.

- We achieved certification as a 100% domestic services provider through The Foundation for Transparency in Offshoring.

7. Finally, see if one or two of the Superior Benefits statements qualify as Unique Advantages for you. These are brand promises that none of your competitors can match at your level.

Here's an example of a **Unique Advantage**:

1. We are the only outsourced call center in the country to be ISO 27001 certified, and we're PCI compliant.

www.thewhalehunters.com
© 2007-2016 The Whale Hunters, Inc.

info@thewhalehunters.com

When you lead your team through this exercise, everyone will be keenly aware of how your marketing statements compare to those of your competitors. You will have a roadmap of claims that you need to challenge, claims that you need to enhance, and claims with which you should lead. You will have a list of brand promises to translate into customer benefits, and for which you can develop new and more compelling evidence to present to customers.

Visit our website now to claim your free list of 50 sample criteria to define your ideal customers!
http://thewhalehunters.com/ideal

info@thewhalehunters.com
www.thewhalehunters.com
© 2007-2016 The Whale Hunters, Inc.

Reflection

To reflect on this chapter, complete the first part of your brand audit—identifying brand promise statements from your company and your competitors.

List the brand promises below (or put each one on a sticky note on a white board)

Brand Promises

-
-
-
-
-
-
-
-
-
-
-
-
-

28

Action

Sort the brand promise statements into three categories:

1. Standard promise

2. Superior promise

3. Unique advantage

Does your company have any superior promise statements?

_____

_____

_____

_____

Do you have any unique advantage statements?

_____

_____

_____

_____

If not, work with your sales and marketing team to better define what promises are represented by your products and services.

If you're not sure, ask your customers to help. Send them a survey or give them a call. Your mastermind group, board of advisors, or other friends can assist as well.

When your company is growing rapidly, what was "true" yesterday is no longer "true" today. To make way for "truly" transformational growth, you must cast aside old notions of "truth" and open your mind to new possibilities.

30

Killing the Truth

You've heard it said that all learning begins with telling the truth. Well, I'm here to tell you that some learning begins killing the truth.

When you make a commitment to transformational change in your company, you have made a commitment to learning. Less obvious but equally important, you've made a commitment to "unlearning" – to killing "the truth."

How many times do you hear these phrases in a business meeting?

- "To tell you the truth..."
- "If the truth be known..."
- "The real truth is..."
- "Just face up to the truth."

And how often do you respond with a contrary "truth" of your own? In a meeting of five honest people, you may learn five different truths. But sometimes "the truth" is just another dodge to impede progress.

Consider five reasons to kill the truth.

1. **"The truth" speaks to the past.** For years, Americans scoffed at products "made in Japan." According to "the truth," Japanese products were inferior to our own. But failure to revise that truth for the future cost Detroit its world and domestic dominance of the auto market. America's market share continues to decline in the face of Japanese quality and value.

www.thewhalehunters.com
© 2007-2016 The Whale Hunters, Inc.

2. **"The truth" reinforces myths.** One of the oldest western myths is caveat emptor, "let the buyer beware." That one seemed to be true for centuries. But the Internet has given global buyers an exponential increase in access to critical information. Today, sellers are subordinate to buyers who can shop around the world for the best value proposition.

3. **"The truth" ignores context.** Andrew Grove told the story of what happened when Intel released with great fanfare a new microchip. Soon after, a mathematics professor claimed that the chip had an esoteric bug – a bug that would confound only one in millions of calculations, but a bug nevertheless. Popular media went to town with that story. Intel, a B-to-B company, had never interacted with end users. But its "Intel Inside" branding strategy had suddenly created a new context – a direct-to-consumer brand – which caused computer buyers to come straight to Intel for satisfaction about the faulty chip.

4. **"The truth" dampens debate.** We've seen decades of "truthful" prognostications about invention and innovation. Television will ruin the minds of our youth. Electronic calculators will destroy mathematics. Personal computers will undermine the writing process. Cell phones will destroy civility. Perhaps any of these statements is "the truth" to you. But if so, there's no conversation and no opportunity to learn.

5. **"The truth" privileges hierarchy.** Who gets to declare "the truth"? For most of human history, and for many areas of the world today, "the truth" is not derived by collective reflection and decision-making among the people. Rather, it is a fiat enforced by economic, military, religious, and political power. To be successful in today's business environment, in contrast, leaders need to call on the collaborative talents and skills of employees who bring to the table a diversity of "truths" that spark everyone's imagination and creativity.

Culture is the shared history of what works. If your company is not achieving the growth and profitability that you want, you can be sure that some things that used to work simply don't work anymore.

We challenge you to kill "the truth" to make way for transformational growth.

Reflection

Brainstorm with your team. What "truths" do we sometimes express or act upon that may no longer be true?

-
-
-
-
-
-

Starting with #1, the most important, rank these statements in order of their importance to your future progress. Which ones will make the biggest difference if you focus on "killing" them?

-
-
-
-
-
-

34

Action

From the previous REFLECTION activity, write your five most important truths that you need to unlearn. Work with your team to identify ways to work on your unlearning, and assign a champion to be in charge of each one.

"Truth" to be Killed	How to Do It	Champion

35

To win the race, you've got to run faster than your competitors. But how much faster than your market's rate of growth do you want to grow? To outrun your competitors and revolutionize your industry's standards, hunt whales.

www.thewhalehunters.com
© 2007-2016 The Whale Hunters, Inc.

info@thewhalehunters.com

Whale Hunting and Wealth Management

You're bumping your head against a rubber ceiling. When it's hot, the ceiling expands and allows you to grow. When it's cold, it contracts, and the brittle surface inflicts bruises and forces you down. You own a thermometer but you can't control the thermostat.

Many of our clients struggle with the stop-and-go, feast-or-famine syndromes of growth. We promote whale hunting to overcome the uncertainty, to break through the ceiling, and to increase predictability. The CEOs ask us, "How much of my business should be whale hunting?"

Our answer is another question: "How much faster than your market's rate of growth do you want to grow?" Whale hunting promises fast growth. If you want to grow faster than you have grown, if you want to grow faster than your competitors are growing, hunting whales offers a unique advantage.

Think of whale hunting as one component in a balanced investment strategy. It's often illustrated as a pyramid. The base of the pyramid includes "low risk-low return" investments that chug along without a lot of ups or downs in their returns. Think of these as smaller accounts that you have had a long time or that your routine branding and marketing activities generate at a regular rate.

The middle portion of the pyramid has more fluctuation but offers higher returns. Think of these as mid-size accounts that you acquire through direct sales efforts by your sales team or through a sales channel.

info@thewhalehunters.com

www.thewhalehunters.com
© 2007-2016 The Whale Hunters, Inc.

The apex of the pyramid is the "high risk-high reward" segment of your strategy. Whale hunting happens at this level.

Imagine a line between the middle and high points in the investment pyramid. Everything below this line will grow your business at a market standard for growth in your industry.

We mean that your competitors are achieving the same levels of growth that you are, by doing the same things you are doing. Like you, your competitors are taking positive steps to improve sales, such as:

- Beefing up the sales staff – swapping out low performers for higher performers

- Betting on sales management – hiring a business development manager

- Implementing sales tools – CRM, contact management, sales kits, and demos

- Buying sales training – investing in the performance of current sales personnel

In this universe, you will achieve some incremental advantage for a while. Your competitors will pass you for a while. Back and forth it will go, each of you achieving a bigger or smaller slice of the standard market pie.

Whale hunting is the only way to grow your business aggressively above the market rate.

www.thewhalehunters.com
© 2007-2016 The Whale Hunters, Inc.

info@thewhalehunters.com

If you choose to become a whale hunter, you will leave your competitors wading in the low tide. You, on the other hand, will be riding the big waves because you will:

- Set the rate of "market rate plus" growth by defining in advance what size of accounts you want to hunt and how much business you want from them. We call that process "Chart the Waters."

- Develop an investment strategy to allocate your resources to achieve the amount of growth you want. You will balance your business with small and mid-size accounts to support your market rate growth while you hunt whales to fuel your maximum growth potential. We call that process "Plan the Hunt."

- Predict with greater accuracy the speed of business acquisition, plotting a longer range growth strategy. We call that process "Manage the Hunt."

- Develop a process to maximize the opportunities from your current whales, about which you know more. You can balance your risk appetite with knowledge so that your whale growth is less risky. We call that process "Searching for Ambergris."

You've heard the adage that says, "Give a man a fish and he'll eat for a day. But teach him to fish and he'll eat for a lifetime." Whale hunting revolutionizes the fishing industry! Whale hunting is not about besting your competitors. That's a limited goal that will produce at best a consistent, incremental advantage in your market. It will never produce rapid growth.

info@thewhalehunters.com
www.thewhalehunters.com
© 2007-2016 The Whale Hunters, Inc.

Whale hunting changes the game. Whale hunting focuses your attention on growth that surpasses your competition to the point that they are no longer computed in your business equations.

Are you ready to update your business growth investment portfolio and change the game?

Reflection

Here is the percentage of my current accounts that fall into each category:

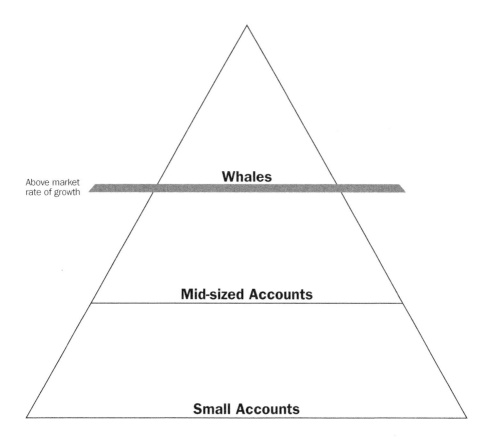

Above market
rate of growth

Whales

Mid-sized Accounts

Small Accounts

info@thewhalehunters.com

www.thewhalehunters.com

Action

Here are some ways that my company could safely start to work on larger account.

☐ [Name] salesperson could devote _____% of time to whale hunting. He/she could handle _____ account(s) at a time. [e.g. 1 whale account, 3 whale accounts]

☐ Each salesperson could handle _____whale account(s) at a time in addition to current accounts.

☐ We could skip one tradeshow (_____) and devote our savings to large account hunting.

☐ Work on getting new business from our current large accounts.

☐ Other solutions:

Here are my top two ideas and how I am going to handle them:

Strategy	Detail	Who is Responsible
New business from large accounts	Start with Acme Tools account	Rafael, current account sales rep

Frank Sinatra made famous the song "I only have eyes for you." Frank was singing about a woman, of course. But it's a good song for whale hunters, who need to have eyes not on a single whale, but on their vision of the ideal.

Define Your Idea Customer

The Whale Hunters believe that companies should decide deliberately which large companies they want to do business with and are well-suited to serve. Rather than sending a message to the entire market and waiting for leads, whale hunting helps you develop a list of companies that you can research, follow, and learn how to approach. This work begins with developing a Target Filter, a set of criteria for your ideal customers

The first step in building your Target Filter is to determine the categories of your criteria–not the metrics (they come next) but the criteria themselves. That is, categories like

- Size of the company
- Geographic Location
- Annual Revenue
- Incumbent Provider of What We Sell
- Reputation

- Financial Stability
- Leadership Team
- Source of our Lead
- Budget for our Product/Service

Every whale hunting company will have a different set of categories that are important to you. Sit down with your leadership team and a whiteboard to define the categories that matter to you. Argue about them! Test them against your current or past customers.

The next step is to add measurable numbers, statements, or qualities that will help you separate the best whales from the rest. You should develop three columns of metrics for each category: A, B, and C. The "A" category is the ideal and the "C" category is the lowest metric that would be acceptable if other things about the company and the sale were right. The "B" category is in between those extremes.

Here are some examples of metrics:

Numbers:

- company revenue: In the "A" category, revenue should exceed $800 million in annual sales; in the "C" category, revenue should exceed $100 million

- deal size: In the "A" category, the potential deal size would exceed $500k; in the "C" category, deal size would be above $100k

Statements:

- brand recognition: In the "A" category, the statement is high quality internationally known brand; in the "C" category, the statement is high quality brand not yet well known.

- growth plan: In the "A" category, the statement is aggressive growth plan; in the "C" category, the statement is incremental growth plan.

Qualities:

- fiscal soundness: In the "A" category the quality is exceptional; in the C category the quality is average.

- geographic location: In the "A" category the quality is western U.S.; in the "C" category the quality is international.

Please note that all of the metrics, statements, and qualities will be different for each company and each target filter. These are YOUR criteria for finding the best sales prospects.

Once you have worked through the metrics with your sales and business development team, you need to test them with past and current customers to be sure they are realistic markers of what is ideal for you. The discussion—even argument–around metrics is healthy and will lead to new understandings.

The metrics may change over time. Make them part of your strategic planning process to ensure regular review and updating.

And above all, once you've determined metrics–manage to them! If a prospect or a prospective deal does not meet your criteria, walk away!

46

Reflection

Based on this chapter, work with your team to create a Target Filter to define your Ideal Customer.

Category	A Metric "3 Points"	B Metric "2 Points"	C Metric "1 Point"

47

Action

Take your new Target Filter and use it to analyze your current (or previous) biggest accounts. Score each account by awarding a 3, 2, or 1 in each category. Then add the total points. Ask these questions about your accounts:

1. Do they meet any of your criteria? If not, work more on your metrics.

2. Are your criteria reasonable or just a pipe dream? If unrealistic, tweak them.

3. When you enter key criteria into a business database (try manta.com for free online, or go to Research USA at your local college or public library), do you get names of companies that you would like to do business with?

4. Can you identify no more than ten categories/metrics that would make for a great client?

5. Will these criteria help you say NO to some deals that you should no longer be investing time in? If not, keep working on the metrics in your "C" column. There needs to be a point at which you would walk away from a prospective deal.

www.thewhalehunters.com
© 2007-2016 The Whale Hunters, Inc.

info@thewhalehunters.com

Scouting, hunting, and harvesting whales require "all hands on deck," both on the boat and back in the village. When in pursuit of whales, always remember this: focus on the hunt, not the hunter. Slackers and heroes need not apply.

info@thewhalehunters.com
www.thewhalehunters.com
© 2007-2016 The Whale Hunters, Inc.

Focus on the Hunt

We've learned a lot about whale hunting by contrasting it with buffalo hunting.

In a buffalo hunt, one brave hunted one buffalo. Yes, many braves charged over the hill at the herd, and others spooked the herd to run, but it was only nominally a team effort. The village celebrated the brave who was most successful: he had the best horse, the least fear, and the most stamina, among other qualities. And if that brave encountered disaster in the hunt, the village suffered terribly from his loss. Buffalo hunting was a hero model.

What does that mean to your company?

In their founding stages, entrepreneurial companies tend to emulate the buffalo hunt. Typically one of the founders is a buffalo hunter – a man or woman whose personal charisma, drive, and knowledge enable him or her to find and close deals. As the company grows, the founder tries to attract heroic salespeople and equip them to replicate his or her expertise. Absent the entrepreneur's unique ability, however, the second-generation buffalo hunters too often fail at heroics.

Even more important, your leadership team begins to fear that the methods of the buffalo hunt don't work to hunt bigger clients and land bigger deals.

In contrast, whale hunting is a collaborative leadership model. Landing and harvesting a whale are far too complex to be left to the expertise of a single hunter. The Inuit whale hunters learned how to organize the resources of their entire village to engage everyone in the annual hunt for whales.

50

Whales do not graze in enormous herds. You can't frighten them into a stampede and pick them off one by one. Whales are smarter, more elusive, more independent, and more complex than buffalo. Your village hunts and harvests whales through replicable process, not individual heroics.

The entire boat went out to hunt, capture, and beach a whale. Think about it: teams of men set out in paddle boats to capture the world's largest mammal! They had confidence, for sure – and moxie, unquestionably – but they also had a replicable process. Equally important, the entire village was needed to harvest the whale. Whenever the whale was beached, that was the time for harvest. No procrastination, no excuses.

As you prepare to "Focus on the Hunt," ask these questions in your company:

- Do you focus on the hunt or the hunter?

- Do you send a boat or a brave to capture a whale?

- Is your sales strategy built on process or heroics?

- Can you harvest the next whale that you capture?

51

www.thewhalehunters.com

Reflection

Here are the ways in which my company behaves like buffalo hunters:

_____

_____

_____

_____

_____

_____

_____

_____

Here are the ways in which my company behaves like whale hunters:

_____

_____

_____

_____

_____

_____

_____

_____

www.thewhalehunters.com
© 2007-2016 The Whale Hunters, Inc.   info@thewhalehunters.com

Action

Here are the three most important ways that we could begin acting more like whale hunters for a large account sale:

Whale Hunting Behavior	Actions Needed	Responsible Person	Due Date for Action

www.thewhalehunters.com

Inuit whale hunters knew the importance of striking the balance between the hunters' ability to capture a whale and the village's ability to harvest it. Commitment to communication, cooperation, and contribution ensured a steady diet of whales.

54

info@thewhalehunters.com

The Village Teeter-Totter

We all recall playing on a teeter-totter as kids. If the weight at each end were evenly balanced, you and your partner could work together to enjoy the ride. But if one partner were too heavy, his or her end would crash to the ground and the other partner would be up in the air, flailing around and unable to land.

The Inuit whale hunters did not play on teeter-totters, but they did know the importance of maintaining the balance between the hunters' ability to capture a whale and the village's ability to harvest it. That's why they trained everyone in their village, from the age of four, to help in harvesting the whale.

When their scouts reported that the boat was bringing a whale to the beach, the villagers gathered all of their people and all of their tools – knives, kettles, firewood, sleds – and raced to the landing spot. They knew that they had a limited amount of time and resources to harvest the whale before it rotted or washed back to sea. Each person knew exactly what he or she was supposed to do, and when to do it, to be the most efficient at harvesting the whale. There was a kind of ultimate accountability, since the village Chief divided the wealth according to each family's contribution.

As a fast-growth company deciding to hunt whales as a way of life, it is critical that you keep your eyes on both ends of your village's teeter-totter to make certain that the partners are balanced. One of your worst mistakes is to beach a whale that your village is not prepared to harvest.

info@thewhalehunters.com

www.thewhalehunters.com
© 2007-2016 The Whale Hunters, Inc.

Three key elements influence your ability to balance the teeter-totter.

1. Capacity. Can your company harvest a whale? You cannot harvest whales until your village has the capacity to do so. We define "capacity" not just by the number of machines you have or the number of people you employ or even the shifts that can be run. Capacity also has to do with your flexibility in organizing resources to harvest each new whale. Therefore, we define capacity as the interaction between two variables: collaboration and resources. You will increase your capacity to harvest as you increase your employees' ability to collaborate across divisional and departmental lines; and as you demonstrate that top management can and will provide sufficient resources and organize resources to meet the harvest demands.

2. Velocity. How fast can you process a whale? Most growing companies have internal practices that get in their own way. Identify and fix the top three internal bottlenecks in your harvesting process that frustrate whales or slow down your ramp. When those are improved, go on to the next three. Pay special attention to the flow of work between departments as well as internal department and divisional practices.

3. Scalability. How many whales can you hunt and harvest each year? Hunting whales requires that your company grow in order to harvest. Focus on the fast-growth characteristics – cross-functional collaboration and flexible resource allocation – and you will ensure your ability to grow.

Understanding these key elements, how do you begin to balance the teeter-totter?

- Before you launch a boat, meet with everyone in your village who will be responsible for harvesting the whale. Include subject matter experts (SMEs) from every department and every activity throughout your operation.

- Simulate how you will respond when you receive a whale-sized order of 10 to 20 times normal.

- Ask each department what it will need, in terms of knowledge, personnel, equipment, logistics, planning, and control in order to harvest the whale.

- Help departments focus on how to organize the village by allocating the available resources in the most efficient ways.

- Follow-through to develop an action plan to prepare each department to handle the next whale.

It will take time to help your employees comprehend the magnitude of what you are planning. And it will take serious thought and investigation on their part to formulate sound answers to your questions.

For a long-lasting teeter-totter, help your departments make plans for harvesting whales as a steady diet.

Reflection

Here is how I rank my company on capacity, scalability, and velocity, with "1" being "outstanding" and "5" being "very weak." Below each capacity I have identified reasons for my selection.

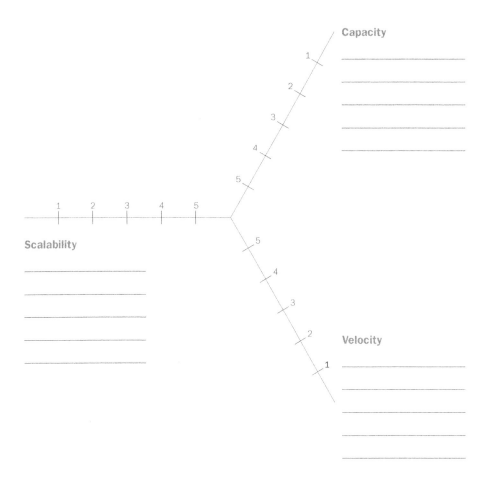

Action

Here is my action plan to improve where needed to be able to handle a whale hunt.

	Actions Needed	Due Dates
Capacity		
Scalability		
Velocity		

www.thewhalehunters.com
© 2007-2016 The Whale Hunters, Inc.

One definition of "empathy" is the ability to put yourself in someone else's position, to experience their thoughts and feeling. Empathy is a remarkable skill for sellers, and in this chapter we talk about how to think like the buyers do.

60

How to Think Like a Buyer

I love to talk to buyers – purchasing agents, procurement officers, brand managers, you name it – and I love to invite them to talk with our clients at The Whale Hunters workshops. The more we talk to buyers and understand their world, the more effective we become in closing sales to the big companies or agencies or foundations that they represent.

In recent workshops and Expert Series calls, we have been fortunate to have whale representatives in the room who are or have been buyers for large organizations in the private, pubic, and nonprofit sectors. I've distilled their advice below.

- Buyers are happy to meet with you under the appropriate circumstances- that is, before an RFP comes out, not when they are in the process; and when you are ready to have a specific, pertinent discussion, not a scavenger hunt. Their job is to make good decisions on behalf of their company or organization; the more they know suppliers, the easier their job becomes and the more successful they can be.

- Do your research. The buyers are the key conduits to the end users at the their big company or government agency. Research their company, their current suppliers, their personal business profiles and past experience.

- Meet the buyers before it is opportunistic. They are much freer to interact with you when they are not in the middle of a solicitation to which you are responding.

- Prepare for your meeting. Know what they buy and ask specific, pertinent questions about how you might be able to meet their needs.

info@thewhalehunters.com

www.thewhalehunters.com
© 2007-2016 The Whale Hunters, Inc.

- Practice courtesy and good staging. Show up on time; leave promptly. Find out who will be in the meeting before you arrive. Know their names, titles, and roles.

- Be memorable: Leave brief, pertinent info about your company with simple points of contact.

Buyers network too!

- They prefer to do business with people they know and like who have performed well in the past. Directing business to those companies means one less set of problems to deal with. If you are a newly registered/ approved provider or have been named to a preferred vendor list, keep your name in front of the buyers until they give you an opportunity.

- Ask buyers who know you to introduce you to others in different organizations or at different levels. People who buy similar products and services know each other and share information about who's doing good work.

- Therefore it goes without saying that you should do good work, always. Avoid bidding on jobs for which you may be ill-prepared or partnering with others who do not have the same high standards as you. It's extremely difficult to overcome a bad reputation. Perform outstanding work!

Give the buyers what they want.

- It is futile to try to force your services into a bad fit like Cinderella's stepsisters forcing their big feet into her delicate glass slipper. But buyers get very tired of receiving proposals that sound like these:

  - "I can't quite do that, but I do this really well!"
  - "I don't really like your format so I changed it."
  - "You may think you need this, but you really need that."

- The truth is, buyers can buy what they and the people they work with want and perceive that they need. They don't appreciate being treated as if they don't know their business well enough to know what they want. If you know them and build great relationships, you can help them get what they want. Until you have that relationship, the rule is to follow their rules.

- If you don't have enough respect to follow their rules, which may seem trivial to you but meet real needs for them, how will they trust you to follow the rules of an engagement?

Treat the buyers like respected large accounts.

- Be able to discuss how they meet your target filter. Let them know why you've come to them, what you have learned about them, what are the additional things you are hoping to learn.

- Assess the "whale fears" (what would scare them about doing business with a much smaller company) and prepare simple, clear materials to overcome doubts.

- Ask great questions. Be certain that you can ask great questions about their processes, procedures, contracts, financial/reporting requirements etc. Great questions are <u>informed</u> questions.

- Listen! The introductory meeting with a buyer is not a sales call. It is a relationship call, a scouting opportunity. Resist the opportunity to tell everything you know about your company and your products and services. Listen and learn.

It's like a matchmaking service. The buyers and the sellers define their profiles - this is who I am and this is what I am looking for. The closer the match, the better the opportunity becomes for each potential partner. When you are strategic about meeting buyers, you will close more sales to bigger customers.

Visit our website now to claim your free list of 50 sample criteria to define your ideal customers!
http://thewhalehunters.com/ideal

Reflection

In a whale-sized account, several or even many individuals will be part of the buying team—that is, people who influence the decision to buy. Some of their titles are identified below. Next to each title, identify an approach or an action that you think they would respect and another approach or action that you think they would reject.[If a title is irrelevant to your product/service, just skip it].

Title	Respect	Reject
(Example) Director of Human Resources	Ask her how she rolls out new training in her company.	Ignore her because she isn't in charge of buying.
IT Director		
COO		
Purchasing Agent		
Key End User for your Product/Service		
Legal Counsel		
Supply Chain Manager		
Director of Customer Service		
Sales VP		
Consultant managing the procurement process		
Customer Service Manager		
VP of Marketing		
Plant Manager		

www.thewhalehunters.com
info@thewhalehunters.com   © 2007-2016 The Whale Hunters, Inc.

Action

Based on your reflection on the previous worksheet, identify 3 key things your should begin to do and 3 key things your team should discontinue doing in their interactions with buyers.

NEW THINGS TO DO:

THINGS TO DISCONTINUE:

66

Like the whales that migrate from south to north each spring, your company's whales have "seasons," too. Know your whales! But be prepared: you will have to send them back to Baja if they migrate beyond your reach.

Back to Baja

How long will you pursue a deal?

Do you understand the metrics of your sales cycle well enough to know when you've missed the opportunity for now?

Can you send a whale "Back to Baja"?

Take a lesson from the Inuit of the far northwest, who early each spring hunted whales that migrated from Baja, California, to the cooler summer waters of Alaska. Year after year, the same pods of whales migrated north for the summer and returned south for the winter. The Inuit were expert scouts who knew the signs that preceded the whales' arrival. The village did not expect to land all of the whales each year. They focused all their energies on landing and harvesting one whale, and they let the rest go back to Baja.

Whale-sized customers have similar traits. They have cycles and seasons of buying. If they get a little too far north, you will not capture them this year. It's imperative to know when you've missed the whale for the current cycle. Hunting whales that are out of reach for this season is a fruitless endeavor that puts the village's survival at risk.

Sending the whale back to Baja is not just good sales practice – it is an essential business management practice for fast-growth companies. You can build your business exponentially by scouting, harpooning, and harvesting a steady diet of whales. But to do this, you need to study, learn, and document your whales' migration patterns. That means:

- Know your whales and understand their buying seasons and cycles

- Scout your ocean to find signs of readiness long before the whale arrives

- Launch your boat in advance of the whale's arrival

- Understand when the whale has migrated beyond your reach

This last point is the hardest to implement. Once you have a whale on your horizon, your harpooners will want to continue the hunt. But the hunt is costly and dangerous, so smart villages focus on the whale's 90-year lifespan. Once the whales have passed for this year, the villagers begin to prepare for the next migratory season.

Whale-sized corporations around the world conduct business with small companies. But they buy on their own time and their own terms. The wise village learns the habits of its whales and knows when to send them back to Baja to hunt next year.

Should any of your whales be sent back to Baja?

69

REFLECTION

Brainstorm with your team:

1. Here are some deals from the past that we pursued too long.

2. Here are some current deals that we should probably give up on for now.

3. Here are the things (I/WE) do that encourage our team to keep pursuing a deal even when they believe it's dead?

70

ACTION

1. Here is my list of signs that one of our whales might be ready to buy:

2. Here is my list of signs that the whale is no longer interested right now:

My action plan is to empower ME and MY TEAM to make good decisions about when to pursue and when to send a whale back to Baja!

www.thewhalehunters.com
© 2007-2016 The Whale Hunters, Inc.

The King of Rock-n-Roll lives on in legend. But there is no place for the Rock Star salesperson in your company. You need salespeople with fearlessness, focus, facilitation skills, impeccability, and patience. We call them "harpooners.".

72

Elvis is Dead
I know that you have done the gas-station-double-take:

"Is that...? I mean he looks just like... NO, it couldn't be... maybe..."Maybe you also operate under the flawed belief that you are going to find the "Elvis of Sales" for your industry and recruit him or her to be the Rock Star salesperson for your company... maybe... well...

I am here to tell you, in the strictest of confidentiality: the King is dead.

Companies that want to grow rapidly often make the Rock Star mistake when they try to hunt whales. Hiring known salespeople who have a track record of success with competitors is often the choice. But I don't recommend it.

You will have three big problems with Rock Stars:

1. **Rolodexes rarely roll.** Big clients with complex needs do not usually follow just one salesperson from company to company – even if those clients want to. The cost of change is high, the integration with the current provider is deep, and the number of touch points beyond the salesperson is broad. For these reasons, if the client relationship has value, it will be hard for the salesperson to move it, no matter what that salesperson may claim.

2. **Prima donna premium.** As Rock Star salespeople develop a larger client base, they naturally create a certain perception of high value to themselves and others. If you recruit them, you will have to pay higher than your current salespeople, more than market rate, and often above reason. The trouble is pay-back. Complex sales usually take a long time before they are realized, so you will be paying a lot for a long time with little to show for it. And if the Rock Star is not as successful as you hoped, you will pay way too much to learn that.

73

3. Circumstances can't be cloned. Although Elvis stood front stage and center, the "Elvis phenomenon" was created by a lot of people and hard work. That one-in-a-million performance occurred not just because of Elvis's vocals, his beguiling sneer, or even his swiveling hips. It was in fact a combination of many people and events working together, perhaps behind the scenes but nevertheless in harmony. The likelihood that your company can recreate the circumstances surrounding a Rock Star's success is low.

So who should you hire?

Remember, The Whale Hunters believe that 90% of success is process. But that still means that 10% is magic. That magic has everything to do with people, including remarkable salespeople. So if you forego the Rock Star, what kind of talent should you seek?

Great whale hunting salespeople ("harpooners") have these qualities:

- **Fearlessness.** These harpooners are not afraid of big companies, big deals, or big competitors. That is a very special talent. It goes beyond being willing to call on these groups or discuss these opportunities or compete against these companies. It means knowing that you and your company are without a doubt worthy. It's not being rash, but believing in the quality of your team.

- **Focus.** These harpooners only work deals they can win, get out of deals early when they can't, and know the difference between the two. Their work is predictable and allows you to plan confidently.

74

- **Facilitation skills.** In the whale-sized deal there are many more steps in the process and more people in the whale and in your company. These harpooners know how to leverage and maximize all of the interactions that happen between their company and the whale. This is less about talking and more about coordinating.

- **Impeccability.** Great harpooners are flawless in preparation, flawless in follow-up, flawless in details, flawless in involving the right people at the right time, and flawless in expressing gratitude.

- **Patience.** A whale hunt takes a long time. There are twists and turns and there are times that it happens with more darkness and fog than sunlight. Great harpooners are confident, so they are patient in the hunt. They don't rush or push when all that energy will get them is a frustrated team. However, once they have the whale on the line, they are relentless in the pursuit.

We all know and admire the Rock Star's allure – her presence, his charisma – and it is very tempting to seek to profit from their talents. But their gifts are narrow, expensive, and impossible to replicate on a new stage. Impersonators are everywhere, but we know that Elvis is dead.

Reflection

Here are my evaluations of my current salespeople on the "suitability for whale hunting" criteria, with "1" meaning outstanding and "5" meaning "needs a ton of work."

Salesperson				
Fearless				
Focused				
Facilitator				
Impeccable				
Patient				
Total				

Low scores are the best. Ideal score is 5. Worst score is 25.

www.thewhalehunters.com
© 2007-2016 The Whale Hunters, Inc.

info@thewhalehunters.com

Action

Here is my action plan for working with the sales team. This will be a series of discussions about qualities of whale hunting sales.

Topic/Date Who	Fearless March	Focused April	Facilitator June	Impeccable	Patient
Fred	✗		✗	✗	

info@thewhalehunters.com

www.thewhalehunters.com
© 2007-2016 The Whale Hunters, Inc.

By involving your company's subject matter experts (SMEs) in your hunt for whales, you not only increase your potential to close large, complex deals, but you ensure a smooth transition from agreement to implementation as well.

78

Balance the Boat

You are the salesperson pitching a big deal to a huge prospect. Seven buyers assemble across the mahogany conference room table, waiting for reasons to say, "No." On your side are yourself and four others from your company – let's say someone from Customer Support, an IT manager, your COO, and an engineer. As your presentation evolves, each member of your team speaks directly, eloquently, and appropriately about his or her role in delivering your products and services to this company. They answer tough questions from their buyer counterparts knowledgeably and with conviction. They make the sale for you, as you knew they would.

Wake up... Chances are you are dreaming.

How good are you at involving subject matter experts (SMEs) in your complex sales?

The Whale Hunters advocate integrating technical resource people into the sales process. In our metaphor, this is "launching the boat." Involving SMEs with their counterpart peers in the whale organization greatly increases your potential to close a large, complex deal. Plus, the time that your SMEs spend with the whale staff pays off big-time in smooth execution of the new agreement.

So why do we find owners, CEOs, and sales managers hesitant to use their own SMEs or the resources of their vendor-partners? In a word: FEAR.

Salespeople fear that SMEs will misspeak because they don't understand how to talk to a client. Owners and CEOs fear a waste of valuable work time from important operational people. SMEs fear taking on more work and being unprepared for a role in the sales process.

www.thewhalehunters.com
© 2007-2016 The Whale Hunters, Inc.

In order to reduce that fear, you have to meet three important criteria:

- Train your SMEs to leverage their unique abilities.

- Plan your hunt to maximize everyone's time.

- Win often to reinforce everyone's confidence in the time and talent investment.

How do you accomplish these three things?

Training – line up your talent. Your boat's responsibility is to give that whale the confidence to make a large purchase from your company. That means the people on the whale's team must learn to trust your people, individually and as a team. In a whale-sized deal, you can develop trust by being "ABLE" in three attributes:

- **Credible.** Explain and discuss the experience and credentials of each oarsman as it relates to delivering your services and/or products. The credibility of each SME is one of your credentials to the whale.

- **Capable.** Demonstrate very specifically your team's knowledge of the whale and the whale's needs. Communicate your company's unique solution to solving the very specific issues of the whale. "Credibility" is all about you, but "capability" is all about the whale.

80

- **Likeable.** In whale-sized relationships, your team will work with the whale over a long period of time. That means that the people on your team should be likeable. A big part of their role is to develop friendly relationships with their counterparts. Be intentional in your selection and coaching of team members to be sure that they can meet the "likeability" test.

Planning – script and rehearse. Never take a boat on a hunt without rehearsal. The only way to have confidence in your boat, and for SMEs to have confidence in themselves is to walk through the meeting in advance.

Every part of the call should be scripted carefully so that each SME has a clear understanding of his or her role and how the entire meeting will unfold. The SMEs should know exactly what to say, when to say it, and when to wait for a cue from the harpooner who is orchestrating the meeting.

If you take SMEs along on the sales call without a specific plan for using them to accomplish one of the three trust areas, you are wasting their time and the company's money. An SME is part of a sales process step for one reason only: to help you close the deal.

Winning – make a big show. Don't go cheap. You do not hunt whales for the exercise; you hunt whales to win and grow. Your whale is likely to bring more than five people to a meeting with your company about a large deal. If you send only one salesperson and perhaps one technical person to the meeting, they will be thinking,

81

"Are they too small to handle us?" or "Do they not get it that this is a big deal?" or "Is this what it will be like to work with this company – everything through a salesperson and none of the real delivery team?"

We use a rule of thumb: "No less than two less." That means that when you are dealing with a whale, take no less than two fewer people to the meeting than the whale will be bringing. If they have seven, you need at least five. If they have five, you need at least three.

Remember, whales focus on safety first. Your team's job is to create a guarantee of safety and reliability. A well-coordinated sales process, leveraging the entire boat, provides that sense of safety and dramatically increases your potential for success.

As your company practices whale hunting by launching a boat powered by the lead harpooner and a team of SME oarsmen, you will experience unprecedented success in closing large and complex sales – the kind that propel your company's growth to new levels. Your subject matter experts will rightfully feel a sense of pride and accomplishment, which they will communicate to their peers on the operational side.

Soon you will find that your company's demonstrated expertise is attracting more whales and earning you seats at even larger tables.

www.thewhalehunters.com
© 2007-2016 The Whale Hunters, Inc.   info@thewhalehunters.com

REFLECTION

Here are the non-sales people in my company who could learn to be part of a large account sale to demonstrate expertise:

NAME   TITLE   CAPABILITIES/EXPERTISE

_____

_____

_____

_____

_____

_____

_____

_____

_____

_____

_____

_____

83

www.thewhalehunters.com
© 2007-2016 The Whale Hunters, Inc.

ACTION

Here are the things I will discuss with my team:

1. Do we have any SMEs who have participated in a sales meeting? How did that work?

2. What SMEs do prospective buyers ask to see (e.g. IT team, Training, Customer Service, Project Management)?

3. What tools would SMEs need in order to participate (e.g. charts, graphs, white papers, website sections?

4. How would we go about preparing for SMEs to participate in a sales call?

5. What is the best way to rehearse for a team presentation?

The Whale Hunters Glossary

The Whale Hunters draw upon the rich legend and lore of the Inuit whale hunters of the far northwest to engage executives in a new way of thinking: for explosive growth, hunt whales.

Ambergris - Rare and priceless substance produced deep within the gut of a sperm whale. The Whale Hunters use this term to represent additional value to be located within existing key accounts.

Beach - During the Beach phase (one of nine in The Whale Hunters Process™), you prepare and present the intake document, develop a harvest map, and commit to performance metrics.

Boat - The team of villagers who hunt and capture a specific whale. The team includes a harpooner, shaman, and several oarsmen, subject matter experts (SMEs) who are needed to close a complex sale. SMEs on each boat represent all areas of the company. The village Chief may also be involved.

Buyers' Table - Those at the whale company who will be affected by your company's solution and participate in the buying decision. Key positions at this table (among others) are the polar bear (economic buyer) and caribou (technical buyers).

Capture - The Capture phase, one of nine in The Whale Hunters Process™, involves those activities traditionally associated with "closing": finalizing the proposal, closing the deal, negotiating terms, and completing the contract.

Caribou - Individuals at the whale company - often technical buyers - who participate at the Buyers' Table and influence the buying decision; however, their position only allows them to say "no."

Chief - President, CEO, Founder or other person identified as responsible for the company's growth and delivery of profits. This person is responsible for ensuring that the village is ready to harvest whales, re-calibrates the Target Filter, and has final say as to whether a boat hunts or not.

Celebrate - During Celebrate (one of nine phases in The Whale Hunters Process™), your company conducts an internal post-harvest review, documents and integrates lessons learned, and determines ways to celebrate the whale (i.e. make the whale aware of both your company's appreciation for it and your company's commitment to your ongoing relationship).

Culture - The shared history of what has made your company successful. As the village transforms into a whale-hunting village, certain cultural beliefs change but core values can be maintained and reinforced.

Dossier (Scouting and Hunting) - Document used to communicate research information about a whale from the scout to the harpooner and shaman.

Eel - Gatekeepers, deal spoilers, and nay-sayers at the whale company who work to prevent any sort of change.

86

Gap Analysis - The results of an analysis the village performs comparing the needs of a particular whale against the village's current ability to meet those needs. Areas such as legal, finance, technology, operations, and logistics are typically included in such analyses.

Harpoon - Harpoon is one of the nine phases in The Whale Hunters Process™. During this phase, the whale hunter gets the whale's attention using a combination of an effective contact approach and a well-crafted message. Your company completes a needs assessment of the whale and designs and delivers a presentation to put forward your credentials and convey your understanding of the whale's needs.

Harpooner - Salesperson who hunts whales. The harpooner is responsible for identifying the key decision-makers inside of a whale, qualifying the whale, generating interest in the whale, and bringing the whale through the sales process.

Harvesting - This term refers to all activities that the boat and the village perform from the point of agreement with a client through a defined period of time (usually the first 90 days of the contract).

Honor - One of nine phases of The Whale Hunters Process™, Honor is the period of time surrounding that point when actual production or service delivery begins.

Intake and Setup - This term refers to specific activities the village and boat perform during the whale harvesting process. These activities are usually focused on an intense period of interaction just prior to the harvest through the first 30 days of contract performance.

Know - One of the nine phases of The Whale Hunters Process™, Know focuses on knowing your market, your strengths, your competition, and the ideal whales that you want to hunt.

Oarsmen - Key subject matter experts (SMEs) who are identified by the shamans and the village Chief to participate in the sales process on the boat. These individuals have specific knowledge of elements of the products/services that the company is selling and contribute to bringing the whale into the boat during The Whale Hunters Process™.

Polar Bear - Target decision-maker (also referred to as the economic buyer) at the whale company who can say "yes" or "no."

Process Map - Visual and narrative representation of the series of choreographed activities in the village's whale hunting process. It includes every element of the nine-phase process - from Knowing the Whale to Celebrating the Whale - in the detailed series of steps that are defined for a particular village.

Raven - Advocates of your company whose wisdom is sought after (and appreciated) by the shaman. Ravens take many shapes and forms. Some ravens are key insiders and associates of your company. Others are your guides on the customer side. Still another type of raven is a compensated intermediary.

Ride - During the Ride phase, you recruit and train subject matter experts to join your hunt, you analyze the whale's buying group, and you stage the whale's visit to your facility. Ride is one of nine phases in The Whale Hunters Process™.

Scout - Marketing person who performs research on whales, generates dossiers on whales, monitors the market for "whale sign," and supports the harpooners as per the shaman's direction.

Searching for Ambergris (SFA) - A specific process and set of tools for capturing more business with the village's existing whale accounts.

Seek - One of nine phases in The Whale Hunters Process™, Seek refers to the process by which your company collects, collates, and tracks account-specific information, including a prospect's readiness to buy. The shaman and harpooners use this information to decide which whales to hunt and how and when to hunt them.

Sew - This phase represents that time between a verbal or even contractual agreement to buy and the actual delivery of services. It is one of nine phases in The Whale Hunters Process™.

Shaman - The direct supervisor of a group of harpooners. The shaman is responsible for training the members of the boat, facilitating the whale hunting process, communicating with the tribe, and managing the tracking process.

Subject Matter Expert (SME) - Villager with responsibilities in hunting and harvesting a specific whale. SMEs represent such areas as research and development, legal, human resources, information technology, operations, manufacturing, shipping, and others. They are selected as oarsmen when a particular boat is launched.

info@thewhalehunters.com

www.thewhalehunters.com
© 2007-2016 The Whale Hunters, Inc.

Target Filter - The target filter is used as the evaluation chart for all prospective whales in the marketplace. Using the elements provided in the target filter, a score is given to each prospect whale and that score determines whether and when the village hunts.

The Whale Hunters Process™ - an integrated sales process by which a company is able to sell and service massive accounts.

Village - All members of the company in all departments.

Whale - A sales prospect for a company that is whale hunting. The prospect is distinct from other sales prospects because it meets pre-defined criteria of size and desirability as a client.

Whale Chart - Environmental scan of the marketplace and its inhabitants. This document identifies and qualifies the various opportunities in the marketplace by their desirable characteristics as a client.

Visit our website now to claim your free list of 50 sample criteria to define your ideal customers!
http://thewhalehunters.com/ideal

Also Available from The Whale Hunters

Whale Hunting is required reading for anyone who is going after the big fish in a market. Engaging, practical, and well organized, it is simply the best book on major account selling out there. Someone once said that confidence is going after Moby Dick in a rowboat and bringing the mayonnaise. *Whale Hunting* gives you the tools to pursue big deals with that kind of confidence.

~ Keith R. McFarland, author of *The Breakthrough Company: How Everyday Companies Become Extraordinary Performers*

The Hunt introduces you to some of the unexpected ways a whale company can slip from the grasp of those small companies that are not able to hold the right tension on the harpoon line. Don't let the whale slip away from you. Learn the ways of the whale, the wind, and the water.

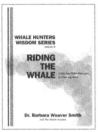

Riding the Whale explains why companies behave the way they do in the middle of your sales process and what you can do about it. In this volume, The Whale Hunters share their experiences and reflect on what it is like to ride the whale to successful completion of the hunt.

Whale Hunting Culture demonstrates that the entire village must be ready to harvest the whale as soon as you beach it— meaning the contract is signed. This volume offers methods to ensure that you can encourage a fast-growth culture that can properly deliver your services to a whale account.

info@thewhalehunters.com

www.thewhalehunters.com
© 2007-2016 The Whale Hunters, Inc.

Whale Hunting with Global Accounts: Four Critical Business Sales Strategies to Win Global Customers

By Dr. Barbara Weaver Smith

Discover the four critical sales strategies to win global customers, whether you're a seasoned global seller or just putting your toes into the ocean, a CEO or a sales manager. Featuring insights from interviews with fourteen global sales practitioners.

*"Barbara Weaver Smith does it again! In her new book, **Whale Hunting with Global Accounts: Four Critical Strategies**, she weaves in foundational concepts from her timeless book, **Whale Hunting: How to Land Big Sales and Transform Your Company** but adds a global bent. By capitalizing on the experience of fourteen experts (I was especially honored to be part of this elite group) she is able to analyze and address the many issues associated with landing and supporting global customers. If your company plans to expand your sales reach into global markets, I would suggest digesting every word of this book – it will save you countless hours and springboard your efforts to building a successful and sustainable global sales program."*

Lisa D. Magnuson
TOP Line Account™ Deal Coach
Top Line Sales

92

Whale Hunters Wisdom, Volume I: Mind of a Hunter

The Whale Hunters
3054 East Bartlett Place
Chandler, AZ 85249
www.thewhalehunters.com
info@thewhalehunters.com

Dr. Barbara Weaver Smith is available to speak to your organization about whale hunting, sales process development and integration, and accelerated cultural transformation. Contact The Whale Hunters at 480.584.4012 for more information.

Printed in Great Britain
by Amazon